Are BANANAS RADIO-ACTIVE?

This edition published in 2022 by Arcturus Publishing Limited
26/27 Bickels Yard, 151-153 Bermondsey Street,
London SE1 3HA

Copyright © Arcturus Holdings Limited

All rights reserved. No part of this publication may be reproduced, stored in a retrieval system, or transmitted, in any form or by any means, electronic, mechanical, photocopying, recording, or otherwise, without prior written permission in accordance with the provisions of the Copyright Act 1956 (as amended). Any person or persons who do any unauthorized act in relation to this publication may be liable to criminal prosecution and civil claims for damages.

Illustrator: Luke Séguin-Magee
Authors: Anne Rooney and William Potter
Editors: Susie Rae and Joe Harris
Designer: Trudi Webb

CH010094NT
Supplier: 10, Date 0622, Print run 00001852

Printed in the UK

CONTENTS

BODY MATTERS 5

LIVING DANGEROUSLY 31

DOWN TO EARTH 51

OUT OF THIS WORLD 75

STRANGE SCIENCE 105

THEY SAY THAT TRUTH IS STRANGER THAN FICTION.

YOU'LL BE ASTONISHED, IMPRESSED, AND EVEN GROSSED OUT BY THE WACKY AND WONDERFUL SCIENCE FACTS COMING UP IN THIS BOOK.

From eating brains and radioactive fruit to pooping in outer space and the strange secrets of a "barking" beach, you'll find plenty to freak out your family and friends. Don't say you haven't been warned!

BODY MATTERS

DO HUMAN BABIES HAVE TAILS?

Before they are born, developing human babies have a tail, and some developing snake babies have legs. Perhaps we have more in common with snakes than we think!

DID YOU KNOW?

In 1945, a woman called Penny Diana Hunter was pregnant for 375 days—making her baby 100 days overdue!

DO SOME PEOPLE HAVE WEBBED FEET?

Being born with webbed hands or feet is quite common. It happens because fingers and toes develop from a flipper-like hand or foot that divides on the unborn baby. If it doesn't divide properly, the skin stays webbed.

WHO HAD 69 BABIES?
In the 1700s, a Russian woman had 69 children: 16 pairs of twins, 7 sets of triplets, and 4 sets of quadruplets. That's a lot of birthdays to remember!

ARE MERMAIDS REAL?
Occasionally, a baby is born with its legs fused together, but still with two feet. This mutation, called sirenomelus, or mermaid syndrome, might have led to stories of mermaids.

HOW RARE ARE TRIPLETS?
One in 10,000 pregnancies results in triplets.

DOES YOUR BRAIN GET SMALLER AS YOU GET OLDER?

No, but your brain gets lighter as you get older. In your twenties, it starts to lose up to 1 g (0.035 ounces) a year as cells die and are not replaced.

CAN YOU MAKE A COMPUTER AS SMART AS THE HUMAN BRAIN?

If scientists could build a brain from computer chips, it would take a million times more power than a real human brain to function.

HOW FAST ARE BRAINWAVES?

Messages are sent to your brain at around 360 km/h (224 mph).

HOW MANY CONNECTIONS ARE THERE IN YOUR BRAIN?

The human brain contains one hundred billion nerve cells. If you could lay out all the possible nerve connections in your brain end to end, they would stretch to about 3.2 million km (2 million mi).

HOW CAN YOU BECOME A BRIGHT SPARK?

The amount of electrical energy generated by your brain is enough to power a small light bulb!

IS EATING BRAINS BAD FOR YOU?

Some of the Fore people of New Guinea suffered from a strange illness that caused shaking, paralysis, and death, defying medical experts for years. It was eventually discovered that the disease, kuru, was caused by eating the undercooked brains of dead relatives, part of the Fore people's burial ritual.

WHAT HAPPENS IF YOU LOSE BLOOD?

Your body destroys or loses 2.5 million red blood cells every second. Luckily, it creates more at the same rate!

WHAT IS THE RAREST BLOOD TYPE?

Only a few hundred people in the world are known to have the rare blood type HH. A person with HH blood can't receive blood transfusions of any other blood type and may need to store their own blood in advance of an operation.

HOW LONG ARE YOUR BLOOD VESSELS?

If all the blood vessels from a human body were laid out end to end, they would stretch 97,000 km (60,273 mi).

HOW FAR DOES BLOOD TRAVEL?

In one day, your blood travels 19,312 km (12,000 mi) around your body!

CAN YOU HEAR THE SEA IN A SEASHELL?

When you hold a seashell to your ear to "hear the sea," what you actually hear is your own blood moving around the blood vessels of your ear.

DID YOU KNOW?

People who live at very high altitudes have blood in their bodies that can deliver oxygen around the body much more efficiently than the blood of sea-level dwellers.

HOW LONG CAN YOU HOLD YOUR BREATH?

Don't try to beat this! The world record for holding a breath is 24 minutes 37 seconds, held by freediver Budimir Šobat from Croatia. Most people can only manage around 1 minute.

CAN SMELLY FEET GIVE YOU BAD BREATH?

If you rubbed garlic on the bottom of your foot, it would be absorbed through your skin and eventually your breath would smell of garlic!

HOW OFTEN DO WE BREATHE?

An adult human takes about 23,000 breaths per day.

WHY ARE TONGUES WHITE IN THE MORNING?

When you look at your tongue first thing in the morning, it is covered in white stuff. These are cells that died during the night.

DID YOU KNOW?

The strongest muscle in your body is your tongue!

DID YOU KNOW?

Girls have more taste buds than boys, and babies have many more taste buds than adults.

HOW CLEAN IS THE HUMAN MOUTH?

There are more bacteria in your mouth than there are people in the whole world!

HOW MUCH SPIT DO YOU MAKE?

You produce about 1 l (2 pt) of saliva every day. It helps to break down your food before you swallow it, and to keep your teeth clean. Every day, you produce enough saliva in your mouth to fill five cups. You will probably produce enough saliva during your life to fill two swimming pools.

HOW IS EARWAX MADE?

There are 1,000–2,000 glands in your ear that produce earwax. The sticky wax collects dirt, dead bugs, and old skin cells before it falls out of your ears. It also kills germs!

WHAT ARE BOOGERS?

Mucus (slime) in your nose collects all the dirt you breathe in, including particles of smoke, pollen, exhaust fumes—and even dust from outer space! The slime and dirt clump together to make boogers.

DID YOU KNOW?
95% of a human's skin is hairy. Some hairs are very fine, though.

WHY DOES READING MAKE YOU TIRED?

If you read a novel that's 100,000 words long (about 400 pages), your eyes will travel just under 1 km (0.62 mi) along the pages.

HOW OFTEN DO YOU BLINK?

Most people spend about the same amount of time blinking as they spend eating—a total of about five years over a whole lifetime.

DID YOU KNOW?

Carrots really do help you see in the dark—they contain vitamin A, which helps the retina to develop.

HOW CAN YOU STOP CRYING OVER CHOPPED ONIONS?

Chewing bread or gum while you peel onions will prevent the onions from making you cry.

WHO CAN SEE SOUNDS?

Synesthesia is a condition that jumbles up how people sense things. They might "see" sounds as shades, or "hear" smells as sounds.

CAN YOU SEE YOURSELF SNEEZE?

No. It's impossible to sneeze with your eyes open.

DID YOU KNOW?

When you sneeze, all of your bodily functions stop momentarily.

IS YOUR APPENDIX USED FOR ANYTHING?

For years, doctors thought the appendix in the gut didn't do anything. But in 2007, scientists discovered that it helps to grow new helpful bacteria if vital bacteria in the gut are killed by illness.

WHO IS THE BEST KISSER—A HUMAN OR A DOG?

You're more likely to get ill from kissing another person than a dog. Even though a dog's mouth has as many germs as a human's, not as many of them are harmful to us.

HOW MANY TIMES DOES YOUR HEART BEAT?

Your heart beats about 42 million times a year.

IS THE PLACENTA AN ORGAN?

Yes. The placenta, which nourishes an unborn baby, is the only organ that develops after a person is fully grown. It is lost when the baby is born and another grows if the woman becomes pregnant again.

DID YOU KNOW?

The placenta uses the same biological tricks as a parasitic worm to hide from the mother's immune system. Without it, the mother's body would reject the baby as an intruder.

DID YOU KNOW?

The human body contains an amazing 10,000,000,000,000,000,000,000,000 atoms.

HOW LONG IS YOUR DNA?

If all of your body's molecules of DNA (the chemical which makes up your genes) were stretched out, they would reach to the Moon and back 1,500 times!

HOW MANY PEOPLE ARE LEFT-HANDED?

Around 10 percent of the population is left-handed, but boys are one-and-a-half times more likely to be left-handed than girls.

DID YOU KNOW?

One in 200 people has an extra rib.

HOW HAIRY ARE YOU?

There are tiny hairs all over your body, except for the palms of your hands and the soles of your feet.

HOW LONG CAN BEARDS GROW?

Beard hair grows faster than any other hair on the human body. If left to grow for his whole life, a man's beard could become 9 m (30 ft) long.

CAN YOU GROW HAIRS ON YOUR TONGUE?

Some people have an abnormality called "hairy tongue" which gives them—you guessed it—a hairy tongue! In fact, it's not hair but extra-long papillae (the little bumps on your tongue). They also turn black!

HOW STRONG IS HAIR?

A single human hair can support the weight of an apple.

WHY DO YOU GET PIMPLES?

A pimple appears when a hair follicle becomes clogged by dried-up oil that oozes out of the skin.

WHAT CAUSES DANDRUFF?

Dandruff is made of clumps of dead skin cells mixed with dirt and oil from your scalp. You lose millions of skin cells each day, so there's plenty available to make dandruff!

WHY DOES ASPARAGUS MAKE YOUR PEE SMELL?

Eating asparagus produces a chemical called asparagusic acid that makes urine smell strongly, although not everyone can smell it.

DID YOU KNOW?

A chemical found in asparagus attracts fish. During the First World War, American soldiers were issued with asparagus so that if they were stranded near water they could eat the asparagus, pee in the water, and catch some fish to eat!

HOW STRONG IS STOMACH ACID?

There is enough acid in the human digestive system to dissolve an iron nail completely.

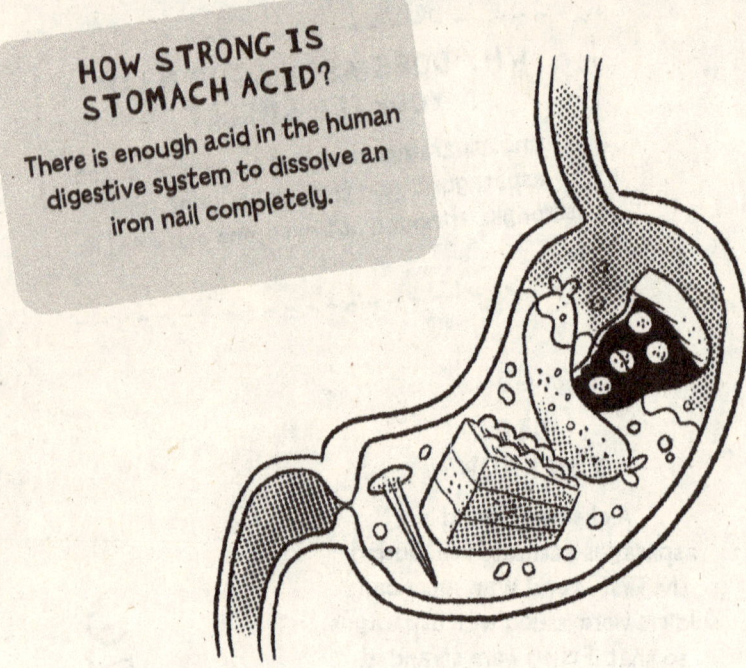

DID YOU KNOW?

Your stomach lining replaces itself every four days.

CAN STOMACH ACID BURN YOU?

Your stomach uses hydrochloric acid to digest your food, but if you spill it on to your skin, it burns you. The stomach produces mucus to protect itself from the acid. When someone dies and the mucus stops, the acid starts to dissolve the stomach.

HOW MUCH DO YOU EAT IN A YEAR?

Every year you will eat about 500 kg (1,100 lb) of food. That's about the same weight as a small car!

HOW MUCH FOOD CAN YOU HOLD IN YOUR STOMACH?

The human stomach can hold up to 4 L (8 pt) of partly-digested food. A cow's stomach can hold ten times as much—enough to fill a whole bathtub!

ARE BANANAS RADIOACTIVE?

Yes, but then most things are to a small extent. The potassium in bananas is a common element, with about 0.012 percent of its atoms being radioactive. But you would need to eat a billion bananas at one sitting to be in any danger.

HOW FAST CAN YOU MAKE A FART?

Gas you take in with food takes between 30 and 45 minutes to be released as a fart. It can come out quicker as a burp. Most people pass about 1 l (2 pt) of gas a day as burps and farts.

HOW MUCH DO YOU POOP?

About 125 g (4.4 oz) of the food you eat each day comes out as poop. Most of the rest is water, and the remainder is nutrients absorbed by your body.

WHY IS POOP SMELLY?

The bad smell of poop comes from chemicals produced by bacteria that break down the food in your gut.

DO OLD PEOPLE HAVE BIG EARS?

Though most of your body will stop growing when you reach adulthood, your ears and nose never stop! This is because they're made of a material called cartilage, which starts to droop and get bigger as we get older.

HOW LONG DO WE SPEND ON THE TOILET?

Over the course of a lifetime, the average person spends an entire year sitting on the toilet. Better bring a book!

DOES SMOKING TURN YOUR LUNGS BLACK?

Yes! Healthy lungs are light pink and have a spongy texture. Smoking cigarettes can turn them black and tarry over time, leading to serious health problems.

DO YOU GROW IN THE NIGHT?

People are taller in the morning than in the evening. During the day, the weight of your body compresses your spine as you walk around, then when you are asleep it expands again.

HOW MUCH SKIN DO YOU GROW IN A LIFETIME?

Your skin is shed and regrown about every 27 days. Most people get through around 1,000 skins in a lifetime.

HOW HEAVY IS SKIN?

Your skin weighs about 3 kg (6.5 lb)—about the same as a brick.

HOW WERE ANTS USED BY DOCTORS?

In ancient times, Indian doctors used live ants to "stitch" wounds together. The doctor would hold the edges together and get the ant to bite through the skin. The ant's head would then be snapped off leaving its jaws as the "stitch!"

WHAT IS A "SOAP MUMMY?"

Sometimes dead bodies remain intact after many years as "soap mummies." This happens when compounds in soil or water speed up a chemical reaction turning fat into wax—which doesn't rot. This bizarre and unusual process is called "saponification."

ARE BRAINS ACTIVE AFTER DEATH?

Electrical activity is detectable in a human brain up to 37 hours after death—but it's not thinking. It's just chemical reactions.

DO HUMANS GLOW?

Believe it or not ... yes, we do! Human beings may not shine as brightly as glowbugs or anglerfish, but we do emit a very small amount of light. We can't see it, because it's 1,000 times dimmer than the light that our eyes can detect.

HOW CAN MAGGOTS SOLVE CRIMES?

Different bugs like to eat dead bodies at different stages of decomposition. Forensic scientists sometimes examine maggots and beetles at a crime scene to work out when a death took place.

DO DEAD PEOPLE FART?

Dead bodies swell up as they rot, because decomposition produces lots of gas. Some dead bodies burp or fart as they release gas, which can be quite alarming!

LIVING DANGEROUSLY

DOES IT EVER RAIN CATS AND DOGS?

No, but there have been rainstorms with falling fish, frogs, and toads! And once, in 1894, a turtle that was frozen inside a giant hailstone fell to Earth.

HOW LARGE CAN HAILSTONES BE?

In 1849, a 6 m (20 ft) block of ice fell from the sky in Scotland as a giant hailstone! In one terrible storm in Bangladesh, 92 people were killed by hailstones that weighed over 1 kg (2.2 lb) each.

CAN IT RAIN BLOOD?

Old tales of a downpour of blood can be explained by red sand being picked up, carried vast distances in clouds, and falling with the rain.

CAN WEATHER MAKE YOU GLOW?

In 1976, children playing in a school football game found that their heads began to glow. It was an appearance of St. Elmo's fire—a glow caused by the build-up of static electricity before a thunderstorm.

WHAT IS BALL LIGHTNING?

Ball lightning is the name given to fiery balls of electricity that whizz through the air, lasting several seconds. No one knows what causes them, and some scientists doubt they exist, even though there have been many sightings. In 1994, ball lightning left a hole in a closed window that measured 5 cm (2 in)!

HOW HOT IS LIGHTNING?

A lightning bolt is five times hotter than the surface of the sun.

HOW TALL ARE CLOUDS?
Some clouds are up to 20,000 m (65,616 ft) thick from top to bottom—more than three times as tall as Mount Everest.

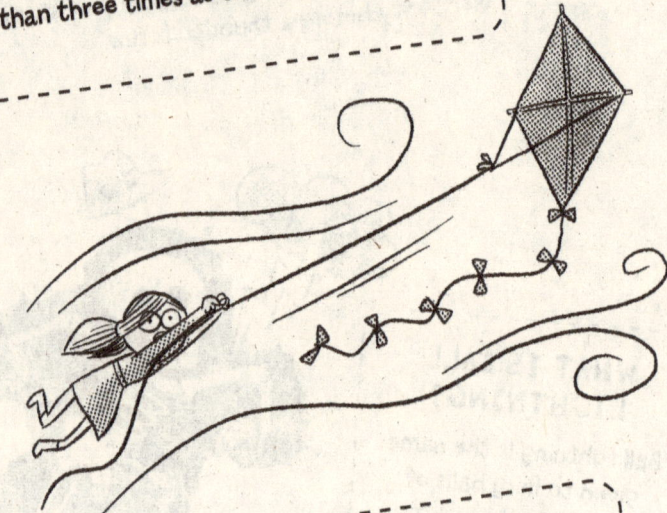

WHERE IS THE WINDIEST PLACE ON EARTH?
Commonwealth Bay in Antarctica has the strongest winds of anywhere in the world—they blow at up to 322 km/h (200 mph).

HOW MUCH WATER IS IN THE CLOUDS?
Only 0.001 percent of the Earth's water is in clouds or falling rain at any one time.

HOW FAST IS RAIN?

A raindrop falls at around 11 km/h (7 mph).

WHERE IS THE RAINIEST PLACE ON EARTH?

Meghalaya in India has 1,187 mm (467 in) of rain a year, making it the rainiest place in the world.

DID YOU KNOW?

The word "hurricane" comes from the name *Huracán*, a Mayan god responsible for storms.

CAN TREES TALK TO EACH OTHER?

Some trees communicate using chemicals. If a wood-eating bug attacks one, the tree releases chemicals into the air, which prompt other trees in the area to produce a poison that deters the bugs.

DID YOU KNOW?

Recycling 1 tonne (2,205 lb) of paper saves 17 trees from being cut down.

WHERE CAN YOU FIND THE TINIEST TREE?

The smallest type of tree is a dwarf willow that grows in Greenland. It is only 5 cm (2 in) tall.

CAN TREES WALK?

The walking or stilt palm walks to a better spot if it doesn't like where it's living! The tree grows up to 20 m (66 ft) tall in the Amazon. Stilts hold it up and support its central trunk. To move, the tree grows more stilts on one side, and then lets the other ones die so that it slowly moves along.

DID YOU KNOW?

There are 1,500 types of insect in a single rain forest tree in the Amazon, including 50 types of ant!

HOW LONG CAN TREES LIVE?

Some trees can live for a very long time. A redwood tree that fell over in California, USA, in 1977 is thought to have been 6,200 years old—which means it started to grow 2,000 years before the earliest human civilizations started.

DO TREES BLEED?

The Australian bloodwood tree oozes red sap that looks like blood when it is cut.

CAN YOU GROW A BRAZIL NUT TREE IN YOUR GARDEN?

Brazil nut trees grow happily in the rain forest environment but refuse to grow anywhere else in the world. Scientists have tried to remove them to cultivate in labs, but the trees don't like it.

DO TREES EMPLOY GUARDS?

Instead of guard dogs, trumpet trees have "guard ants" living in their hollow limbs! In return for their home, the Azteca ants bite anything that nibbles on the tree and then squirt acid into the creature's wound to make it extra sore.

CAN YOU MIX A PLANT WITH AN ANIMAL?

Genetic engineering can combine genes from different plants and animals. A gene from a deep-sea fish can be added to a vegetable to make it frost resistant! Some people call these genetically modified foods "Frankenstein foods."

IS THERE A PLANT THAT LOOKS LIKE POOP?

The anacampseros albissima plant looks like a bird dropping to protect it from being eaten by animals.

DID YOU KNOW?

The pink petticoat plant has a flower that looks like a pretty petticoat—it might look nice, but it gobbles up bugs that crawl inside it.

DO PLANTS GROW IN DEAD BODIES?

Plants often grow inside the skeletons of dead bodies in the Arctic—they make warm homes and have lots of nutrients that nourish plants.

DID YOU KNOW?

A peanut is not really a nut—it grows underground!

WHAT IS THE DOOMSDAY VAULT?

A "doomsday vault" has been built in an Arctic cave to store seeds from all the world's food-giving plants in case a major disaster wipes them all out. It contains more than 860,000 seed samples that should be able to survive for up to 1,000 years.

WHAT PLANTS LOVE TO LIVE ON CORPSES?

Stinging nettles grow well in soil that contains dead bodies—they thrive on a chemical called phosphorous which can be found in the bones.

WHAT IS THE FASTEST GROWING ORGANISM ON EARTH?

Some types of bamboo grow up to 91 cm (36 in) a day. This means they are growing at a rate of 0.00003 km/h (0.00002 mph)! Meanwhile, the veiled lady mushroom grows faster than any other organism in the world. It grows up to 20 cm (8 in) in only 20 minutes, and it can be heard cracking as it grows!

HOW ABOUT A SLOW GROWER?

A cactus that grows in the Arizona desert grows less than 2.5 cm (1 in) in the first ten years of its life. It's a slow starter!

WHAT FLOWER SMELLS LIKE DEAD BODIES?

The corpse flower, or stinking lily, is the smelliest flower in the world. Its stench is disgusting—it smells like a rotting corpse. This attracts insects that feed on the dead matter, and they pollinate the flower.

DO PLANTS EAT BIGGER ANIMALS?

A type of carnivorous plant found in the tropical rain forests of Asia can "eat" birds and even rats. Animals are attracted by the nectar of the flower, and then they fall into a vat of chemicals that dissolve them, feeding the plant.

WHAT PLANT EATS FLIES?

A Venus flytrap is a carnivorous plant that traps and eats flies. It doesn't strike quickly—it takes half an hour to squash a fly and kill it, and another ten days to digest it.

WHAT IS THE WORLD'S MOST POISONOUS PLANT?

The most poisonous plant in the world is the castor bean. Just 70 mg (2 millionths of an ounce) is enough to kill an adult human. It's 12,000 times more poisonous than rattlesnake venom.

WHAT IS THE LARGEST LIVING THING ON EARTH?

In Oregon, USA, is a giant fungus that covers 10 square km (3.86 square mi) underground. It is thought to be around 2,400 years old but may even be up to 8,650 years old.

DID YOU KNOW?

The saguaro cactus can live for up to 200 years and grow to 18 m (59 ft) tall. It stores up to 8 tonnes (16,000 lb) of water inside it—but don't cut one open for a drink in the desert, as it's poisonous to humans!

WHAT IS A WATER DEVIL?

Water devils are small whirlwinds that make thin columns of water that whirl and twist over the surface of a lake. They can look like the neck of a monster, weaving to and fro, and might explain legends of beasts such as the Loch Ness Monster.

DOES IT SNOW UNDERWATER?

The main source of food for animals that live in the deep sea is marine snow—flakes of dead things and poop from creatures who live higher up in the water!

DID YOU KNOW?

Hot water freezes more quickly than cold water.

CAN YOU FIND SEA CREATURES INLAND?

Lake Titicaca, on the border between Bolivia and Peru, is home to lots of sea creatures—but it's an inland lake. The lake was stranded when the landscape changed, trapping sea creatures in its saltwater environment.

DID YOU KNOW?

The oceans provide 99 percent of the habitable space on Earth because they are so deep—on land, all plant and animal life is clustered on the surface.

DID YOU KNOW?

The shell of a lobster is made of chitin—the same substance that mushrooms are made of.

ARE POTATOES POISONOUS?

Potatoes are from the same family of plants as the highly poisonous deadly nightshade. If the potato were to be discovered now, it would probably not be approved as a food!

CAN MUSHROOMS GLOW?

Some fungi glow in the dark and can be seen from 15 m (50 ft) away. They are used as natural lanterns.

IS THE MOON EVER BLUE?

The expression "once in a blue Moon" means that something hardly ever happens. A blue Moon does happen occasionally, though— it happened in 1950 when a large wildfire in Canada sent soot high up into the sky, making the Moon look blue.

HOW TOUGH ARE BACTERIA?

Inside the vents of active volcanoes, bacteria live in conditions equivalent to a vat of hydrochloric acid. They're not fussy about their homes!

WHAT ARE THE NORTHERN LIGHTS?

The aurora borealis, or Northern lights, are displays of swirling green and red light high in the night sky near the North Pole. They're caused by charged particles from the solar wind hitting atoms from the Earth's atmosphere, making them emit light.

WHAT IS THE TUNDRA?

The Arctic tundra is a huge, flat, treeless region that has a permanent layer of frost under the ground. The permafrost is 450 m (1,476 ft) deep underground.

DID YOU KNOW?

If you put a drop of oil into a swimming pool, it will spread over the entire surface until it forms a really thin layer.

HOW OLD ARE CORAL REEFS

Some cold-water coral reefs have been growing since the end of the last ice age—10,000 years ago.

WHERE IS THE COLDEST PLACE ON EARTH?

The coldest place on earth is Vostok in Antarctica, where the temperature falls to nearly minus 90 degrees Celsius (minus 129 degrees Fahrenheit). Unsurprisingly, no one lives there!

WHERE HAS THE LONGEST NIGHT?

The South Pole has no Sun for 182 days each year.

DID YOU KNOW?

In 2001, a geologist in India found fossilized raindrops! The imprint was found in ancient rocks, proving that it rained on Earth 1.6 million years ago.

WHAT DOES RAT POISON TASTE LIKE?

The taste of rat poison varies in different countries. It is adapted to suit the food rats are most used to. Please don't taste it yourself!

HOW BIG ARE BACTERIA?

Most bacteria are tiny—there can be 50 million bacteria in a single drop of liquid. Yet the largest bacterium can just about be seen with the naked eye.

WHERE DID ALL THE ANCIENT ANIMALS GO?

Over 99 percent of all the species in the world that have ever lived are already extinct!

ARE THERE ANY DINOSAURS WE DON'T KNOW ABOUT?

Scientists believe 70 percent of dinosaurs are yet to be discovered, as more new species have been found in the last 20 years than ever before.

CAN YOU EAT MAMMOTHS?

When polar ice melts, it sometimes reveals mammoths frozen since the end of the last ice age. The mammoth meat can still be fresh—on one occasion, dogs ate the defrosted mammoth before scientists could investigate it!

DOWN TO EARTH

HOW THICK IS THE EARTH'S CRUST?

The Earth's crust—the solid surface of the Earth that holds the land and sea—is extremely thin. If the Earth were an apple, the crust would be about as thick as the skin.

IS THE EARTH GETTING FATTER?

Yes! Earth is gradually getting thicker around the middle, becoming more pumpkin-shaped than round.

HOW HOT IS THE MIDDLE OF THE EARTH?

The temperature at the Earth's core can reach 6,000 degrees Celsius (10,800 degrees Fahrenheit).

DOES ALL THE WORLD SPIN AT THE SAME RATE?

No. The Earth's inner core spins more quickly than the outside. Every 900 years, the inner core makes one complete extra revolution compared to the outside. (Not all in one go—it's just going a bit quicker for the whole 900 years!)

WHAT IS THE EARTH'S CORE MADE OF?

The Earth's core is a sphere of metal (mostly iron) about 2,440 km (1,504 mi) across.

HOW FAR UP DOES EARTH'S ATMOSPHERE GO?

The gases of the Earth's atmosphere can reach up to 500 km (311 mi) high!

CAN YOU FIND SEA CREATURES UP MOUNTAINS?

Yes. Fossilized sea animals are often found on the tops of tall mountains. The mountain tops were once parts of the seabed that have been pushed upward by colliding lumps of land.

WHERE IS THE WORLD'S TALLEST MOUNTAIN?

The world's tallest mountain looks quite flat! Mauna Kea in Hawaii is 9,966 m (32,696 ft) tall from its base on the seabed, but more than 50 percent of it is hidden under the sea and the rest doesn't look very pointy!

WHERE IS THE WORLD'S LARGEST MOUNTAIN RANGE?

The largest mountain ranges on Earth are under the sea! They form an area called the mid-ocean ridge, which stretches all around the world, running through the Pacific, Indian, and Atlantic Oceans.

WHERE IS THERE A GREEN BEACH?

Hawaii has a beach with green sand. It's the only one known, and was produced by olivine—a volcanic rock that was smashed into tiny grains.

CAN LIGHTNING MELT SAND?

Yes. When lightning strikes a beach, it melts the sand, which hardens again as a type of glass called fulgurite. It often forms in twisty tube shapes.

WHERE DOES THE BEACH BARK?

A beach in Hawaii is called Barking Sands because the sand seems to "bark" like a dog when it's walked on. The dry grains make a strange sound when rubbed together.

CAN ROCKS FLOAT?

Some rocks float on water. Pumice stone is hardened volcanic lava. It often contains so many air bubbles that it is light enough to float.

WHERE IS THE SALTIEST SEA?

If you lie in the Dead Sea, you float very easily! The sea is nine times as salty as the Mediterranean—too salty for fish to live in—but great to float on! The Dead Sea has amazing healing properties. The water is rich in minerals and helps to relieve skin and joint problems. Don Juan Pond in Antarctica is nearly 18 times as salty as the ocean. It's so salty that heavy objects can float on it, and it remains a liquid down to temperatures of minus 53 degrees Celsius (minus 63.4 degrees Fahrenheit).

HOW OLD IS THE SEABED?

Under the sea, rock moves around slowly and is recycled! It goes back under the surface of the Earth to melt and re-emerges through volcanoes. The entire seabed is renewed every 150-200 million years.

HOW FAST ARE SEA LEVELS RISING?

Glaciers melting and sea temperatures getting warmer have caused global sea levels to rise between 10 and 25 cm (between 4 and 10 in) in the last century. This is all part of global warming.

WHICH IS EARTH'S LARGEST OCEAN?

The Pacific Ocean is the largest ocean on Earth. It covers over 155 million square km (60 million square mi) and has an average depth of nearly 4 km (2.5 mi).

WHERE DOES THE SEA STOP MOVING?

The Sargasso Sea is an area in the Atlantic Ocean that is completely still. Sargassum seaweed has grown over the surface, stopping the water from moving.

HOW POWERFUL IS THE AMAZON RIVER?

Water flows from the Amazon River into the sea with such power that even at a distance of 161 km (100 mi) from the coast, it is possible to scoop up fresh Amazonian water from the sea.

CAN RIVERS FLOW BACKWARD?

Yes. On December 16, 1811, the Mississippi River flowed backward as a result of an earthquake!

WHICH LAKE HAS POISONOUS BURPS?

Lake Nyos in Cameroon, belches out deadly carbon dioxide. Its poisonous burps killed 1,746 people in one night in August 1986. No one really knows where the gas comes from.

HOW CAN MOST OF THE WORLD'S FRESH WATER BE IN THE DESERT?

The largest desert in the world also contains most of the world's fresh water! Antarctica qualifies as a desert as it has virtually no rainfall. The Antarctic ice sheet contains 90 percent of all the fresh water ice on Earth.

DID YOU KNOW?

About one tenth of the Earth's surface is covered in glacial ice.

WHAT ARE ICE CORES FOR?

Ice cores are cylinders of ice that scientists have drilled from the polar ice sheets. They give us information about Earth's climate over the last 740,000 years.

WHAT WOULD HAPPEN IF ALL THE ICE AT THE SOUTH POLE MELTED?

If the entire Antarctic ice sheet were to melt, sea levels would rise by 70 m (230 ft), leaving cities such as New York, Hong Kong, and London completely lost underwater.

DID YOU KNOW?

Lake Vostok lies buried under 4 km (2.5 mi) of ice in Antarctica, but it is full of liquid water. It was last open to the air around half a million years ago and was discovered by radar in 1994.

CAN YOU STEER ICEBERGS?

Small icebergs, fitted with sails, have been steered from the Antarctic to Peru, a distance of 3,862 km (2,400 mi)!

WHAT WAS THE LARGEST-EVER RECORDED VOLCANIC ERUPTION?

One of the largest volcanic eruptions recorded in recent history occurred on the island of Krakatau in Indonesia in 1883. It was so huge that most of the island disappeared into the sea! It made the loudest noise in recorded history—it could be heard hundreds of miles away and the sound waves went around the globe at least three times!

HOW HOT IS LAVA?

The lava (molten rock) that erupts out of a volcano can be as hot as 1,200 degrees Celsius (2,192 degrees Fahrenheit) and the power of a large eruption can equal that of a million nuclear bombs.

COULD MOUNT FUJI ERUPT?

Yes. Mount Fuji is a volcano that towers over the Japanese capital of Tokyo. It last erupted in 1707. The earthquakes and tsunami that followed killed 20,000 people and the rice fields were left barren for 100 years. A major eruption of Mount Fuji is long overdue—it usually erupts about once a century ...

IS THERE A VOLCANO IN YELLOWSTONE PARK?

There is a super volcano underneath Yellowstone Park, USA, that last erupted 640,000 years ago. If it erupted now, ash would be thrown over the entire USA, and the entire world's climate would change—perhaps enough to wipe out humans completely.

DID YOU KNOW?

Scorching hot winds from a volcanic eruption can travel at 300 km/h (185 mph), burning everything in their path at up to 800 degrees Celsius (1,470 degrees Fahrenheit).

ARE THERE VOLCANOES THAT ERUPT NONSTOP?

The Kilauea volcano in Hawaii has been erupting constantly since 1983, throwing out 5 m³ (177 cubic ft) of lava every second!

DID YOU KNOW?

When the Laki volcano in Iceland erupted in 1783, poisonous gas clouds swamped the land, killing half the country's livestock. A fifth of the human population died, too.

DID YOU KNOW?

A volcanic eruption destroyed the Roman city of Pompeii in 79 AD. The energy the eruption released was 100,000 times more powerful than the atomic bomb dropped on Hiroshima, Japan, in 1945.

HOW BIG IS THE SAHARA?

The world's largest hot desert, the Sahara, is almost as big as the USA—it covers nine million square km (3.5 million square mi).

IS THE SAHARA DESERT GROWING?

According to some scientists, the Sahara Desert is growing at a rate of 6 km (3.7 mi) a year.

DID YOU KNOW?

Nearly one-fifth of the Earth's surface is dry desert where less than 25 cm (10 in) of rain falls in a year.

DID YOU KNOW?

The Atacama Desert is so dry that between the years 1964 and 2001, the average rainfall was only 0.5 mm (0.02 in) per year! It had no rain at all for more than 400 years, between 1570 and 1971.

CAN YOU HEAR SAND?

In some deserts, the sand "sings." This eerie sound is produced by the wind moving across the sand.

ARE EGYPT'S PYRAMIDS MOVING?

The pyramids in Egypt have moved about 4 km (2.5 mi) to the south since they were built around 5,000 years ago, because the sand they were built on has shifted.

HOW OFTEN DO MAJOR DISASTERS HAPPEN?

In the last 550 million years, there have been five events that have each destroyed at least 50 percent of all life on the planet.

DID YOU KNOW?

The ninth deadliest natural disaster since the Middle Ages took place in 2004, when a tsunami took place in the Indian Ocean.

WHAT IS A TSUNAMI?

A tsunami is a massive wave that sweeps over the land and destroys everything in its path. A tsunami can travel across the ocean as fast as a jet plane, at speeds of up to 800 km/h (165 mph) and can be 30 m (100 ft) high when it strikes the shore.

HAS EARTH BEEN HIT BY ASTEROIDS?

Yes, many times. A particularly large asteroid or comet created the Vredefort crater in South Africa when it struck Earth two billion years ago. The crater is big enough to fit 270,000 tennis courts inside!

HOW DO YOU MEASURE EARTHQUAKES?

The Richter scale measures the size of an earthquake and goes from 1 (small) to 10 (deadly). The largest earthquake ever recorded was a 9.5 in Chile in 1960. An earthquake measuring 12 would break the Earth in half!

HOW MANY EARTHQUAKES HAPPEN EVERY DAY?

There are 8,000 small earthquakes (measuring less than 2 on the Richter scale) every day—they are too small for people to even feel them.

WHICH CITY IS FIREPROOF?

The city of La Paz in Bolivia is safe from fires—the city is so high up that there is barely enough oxygen to keep a single flame alight.

CAN YOU FIGHT FIRE WITH FIRE?

One method of stopping a wildfire is to start another one! By burning an area ahead of the fire, it's possible to remove the fuel the wildfire needs to keep going.

HOW MUCH ENERGY DOES THE SUN SUPPLY?

Enough energy reaches the Earth from the Sun every second to fulfil all our power needs for a year.

WAS INDIA AN ISLAND?

180 million years ago, India was an island off the coast of Australia. The Earth's land masses slowly move around, at up to 10 cm (4 in) a year, meaning that over millions of years, India gradually moved away from Australia and eventually joined up with the land mass that we now know as Asia.

HOW DO GEYSERS WORK?

Geysers are fountains of hot water, sometimes above boiling point. The water is heated by molten rock under the Earth's crust, and then bubbles back up to the surface under great pressure.

DID YOU KNOW?

Sound travels through granite rock ten times faster than it travels through air.

WHO CROAKED DUE TO CLIMATE CHANGE?

The World Wildlife Fund believes that climate change may have wiped out all the golden toads of Costa Rica—making them one of the first victims of global warming.

DID YOU KNOW?

The Arctic may be totally free of ice for three months each year by 2040 due to global warming. Polar bears could be extinct in 100 years if climate change continues to melt the ice at the North Pole.

WHY IS BEAR POOP IMPORTANT?

Bear poop is an essential part of the North American ecosystem! Grizzly bears eat salmon from the streams and then deposit vital nutrients on the land in the form of droppings and leftover fish.

HOW CAN FOSSILS BE FUELS?

Oil and coal are both made from the dead bodies of animals and plants that lived millions of years ago.

WHAT WAS THE FIRST LIFE ON EARTH LIKE?

During the first 2.7 billion years on Earth, only single cell life forms existed. Then slime molds, sponges, and other very simple forms of life evolved. Everything else has appeared in the past billion years.

WHERE CAN YOU FIND STONES THAT BOUNCE?

Daintree National Park in Australia is famous for its bouncing stones—they can be bounced off each other like balls! It's said that people who steal the stones get cursed ...

WHERE IS THE LOWEST DRY LAND ON EARTH?

The shores of the Dead Sea in the Middle East are the lowest dry land on Earth, at around 420 m (1,372 ft) below sea level.

DID YOU KNOW?
February 1865 is the only month in recorded history to have had no full Moon.

DID YOU KNOW?
The continent of Asia accounts for 30 percent of the Earth's land but is home to 60 percent of the world's population.

WHICH IS THE EMPTIEST CONTINENT?

Antarctica is the only continent with no native people. Around 4,000 scientists live there in the Antarctic summer, and 1,000 in the winter, making it the least densely populated land on Earth.

DID YOU KNOW?

The oldest rocks in the world are nearly four billion years old.

DID YOU KNOW?

Escape velocity—the speed you need to travel to escape Earth's gravity—is 11.2 km/s (6.95 mps).

HOW WAS THE GRAND CANYON MADE?

The Grand Canyon, USA, was created up to 14,000 years ago by the force of water rushing over the rock as the ice melted at the end of the last ice age.

DID YOU KNOW?

There are around 20 billion tonnes (44 million lb) of gold in the oceans, but it is too difficult to extract it!

DID YOU KNOW?

San Francisco and Los Angeles, USA, are moving toward each other at the rate of 5 cm (2 in) a year. They are due to collide in about 15 million years.

OUT OF THIS WORLD

HOW FAR DOES EARTH TRAVEL IN A DAY?

The Earth travels 2.6 million km (1.6 million mi) around the Sun every day.

DID YOU KNOW?

In 2007, scientists used the internet to link up telescopes based in China, Europe, and Australia to create a single telescope spanning half the Earth.

DID YOU KNOW?

Some rocks that you find on Earth are in fact pieces of the planet Mars that have fallen from the sky!

WHERE DID THE MOON COME FROM?

It is thought that the Moon was formed when a planet collided with Earth and knocked off a huge chunk, about 4.5 billion years ago.

WHAT IS LUNAR HAY FEVER?

Some astronauts have suffered from an illness called lunar hay fever caused by breathing in moon dust.

CAN THE MOON AFFECT YOUR WEIGHT?

Yes. When the Moon is directly overhead, you weigh slightly less than at all other times because of the effect of its gravity.

ARE WE SAYING GOODBYE TO THE MOON?

Yes. The Moon is moving away from the Earth at a rate of about 3.78 cm (1.48 inches) a year.

DID YOU KNOW?

It takes approximately 1.3 seconds for light reflected by the Moon to reach Earth.

HOW HOT IS THE MOON?

The temperature of the Moon can change 380 degrees Celsius (500 degrees Fahrenheit) from day to night, as there is no atmosphere to trap the heat of the Sun.

ARE THERE VOLCANOES ON OTHER WORLDS?

Yes. Pele, the largest volcano on Jupiter's moon, Io, erupts to heights 30 times that of Mount Everest. Gas and the other products of the eruption fall over an area the size of France. Elsewhere, Enceladus, a moon of the planet Saturn, has ice volcanoes that erupt water.

WHERE IS THE BIGGEST VOLCANO IN THE SOLAR SYSTEM?

The tallest volcano in the Solar System is called Olympus Mons. Its peak is 27 km (16.78 mi) above the surface of Mars.

HOW MUCH WOULD YOU WEIGH ON MARS?

If you weigh 45 kg (99 lb) on Earth, you would weigh only 17 kg (37 lb) on Mars because of the difference in gravity.

WHAT WAS THE FIRST EARTH MISSION TO VENUS?

The Russian spacecraft, Venera 1, was ahead of its time. It flew to the planet Venus in 1961—seven years before Apollo 7 orbited the Moon.

HOW HOT IS VENUS?

The surface of the planet Venus has an average temperature of 480 degrees Celsius (896 degrees Fahrenheit). It's unlikely to be the first planet humans visit, unless they want a tan ...

COULD LIFE EXIST ON VENUS?

Some scientists think there may be a zone in the atmosphere of Venus, about 50 km (31 mi) above the surface, where life could exist. Don't think in terms of humans or animals, though—they're only expecting to find tiny microorganisms.

HOW BIG IS SATURN COMPARED TO EARTH?

If we could hollow out Saturn, 764 Earths would fit inside it!

DID YOU KNOW?

Saturn is the least dense planet—it could float on water!

DO ALL PLANETS ORBIT STARS?

Some scientists claim they have discovered "rogue planets" which do not orbit any star but wander through space on their own.

CAN WE SEE NEPTUNE IN THE NIGHT SKY?

Neptune can't be seen with the naked eye—you'll need to use a telescope. It was the first planet to have been predicted by mathematical observations rather than actually spotted.

HOW LONG IS A DAY ON NEPTUNE?

A day on Neptune takes only 16 Earth hours, but a Neptune year is 165 Earth years long—so there are around 60,190 days in a year on Neptune.

HOW COLD IS PLUTO?

The temperature on dwarf planet Pluto is thought to be between minus 233 and minus 223 degrees Celsius (minus 387 to minus 369 Fahrenheit). Wrap up warm if you ever visit!

WHICH IS THE BEST PLANET FOR BIRTHDAYS?

The best planet to live on if you want a lot of birthdays is Mercury. A year lasts only 88 days, so when you're 10 on Earth you'd be 41-and-a-half on Mercury! But don't worry—instead of living to around 80 years old, you'd live to be 332!

DID YOU KNOW?

In around a billion years, the Sun will have grown so much that the Earth will be too hot to live on. It will, however, make Pluto pleasantly warm and habitable for a while, before the Sun increases in size even more and eventually dies.

HOW LONG IS A DAY ON MERCURY?

Mercury's day is so long, you'd only get breakfast once every two years! It takes the planet nearly two Earth years to revolve once, so a day takes a whole year and so does a night!

HOW HOT IS THE SUN?

The temperature of the Sun is 6,000 degrees Celsius (10,832 degrees Fahrenheit) on the surface and a scorching 15,000,000 degrees Celsius (27,000,000 degrees Fahrenheit) in the middle. The atmospheric pressure in the middle of the Sun is 340 billion times greater than at sea level on Earth.

IS THE SUN LOSING WEIGHT?

Yes. The Sun loses 3.9 billion kg (4.3 tons) of weight each second.

HOW LONG DOES LIGHT TAKE TO REACH US FROM THE SUN?

It takes about eight minutes for light from the Sun to reach the Earth. So if the Sun went out now, we wouldn't know for eight minutes!

HOW LONG WOULD IT TAKE TO DRIVE TO THE SUN?

If you could drive an ordinary car to the Sun, moving at 80 km/h (50 mph), it would take over 212 years to get there!

HOW BIG IS THE SUN COMPARED TO EARTH?

One hundred and three million Earths would fit inside the Sun!

WHERE WILL WE GO WHEN THE SUN GETS TOO BIG?

To avoid Earth being toasted as the Sun grows, we could move it out toward Pluto. By harnessing energy from a comet, we could gradually move Earth outward, away from the Sun. Some scientists believe we could have moved the Earth 80 million km (50 million mi) in a few billion years' time.

HOW FAST IS THE SOLAR SYSTEM MOVING?

The Solar System travels at 273 km/s (170 mps) around our galaxy, the Milky Way.

HOW OLD IS OUR SOLAR SYSTEM?

Our Solar System is a youngster in the big happy family of the universe—it's only 4.5 billion years old. The oldest stars are around 13 billion years old.

WHAT IS THE LARGEST THING IN THE SOLAR SYSTEM?

The Sun is not the largest thing in the Solar System—the comet Holmes is even bigger. Although the solid part of the comet is only 3.6 km (2.2 mi) across, the coma (the cloud of dust and gas around it) is wider than the Sun.

WHAT IS THE KUIPER BELT?

The Kuiper Belt is a band of leftover debris from the formation of the planets, which circles the Sun beyond the orbit of Neptune. It contains at least 70,000 objects that measure more than 100 km (62 mi) across.

WHAT IS THE OORT CLOUD?

The Oort Cloud is a vast cloud of comets on the very edge of the Solar System. It houses trillions of comets that measure over 1 km (0.62 mi) across. The outer band of the Oort Cloud may be 30,000 times the distance of the Earth from the Sun, from one edge to the other. Although it contains trillions of lumps of rock, it is probably only a few times the mass of the Earth.

DID YOU KNOW?

Around 40,000 tonnes (80 million lb) of meteoric dust hits Earth each year.

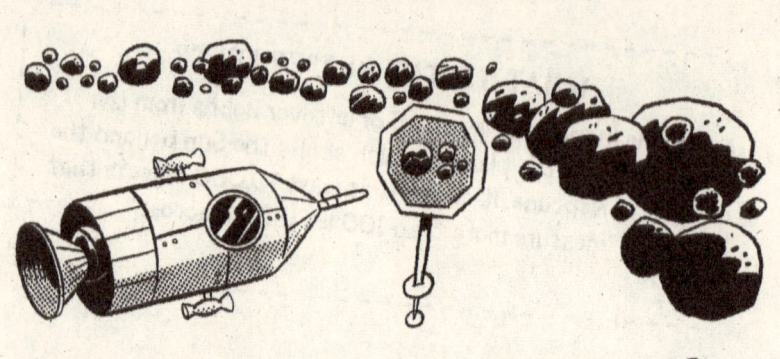

WHAT ARE ASTEROIDS?

Asteroids are small, rocky astronomical objects that orbit the Sun. Hundreds of thousands have been discovered, and they can sometimes behave like planets.

WHAT ARE COMETS AND ASTEROIDS MADE OF?

Comets and asteroids are made from bits and pieces left over from the creation of the Solar System. If someone had tidied up properly, there wouldn't be any!

HOW LONG IS A COMET TAIL?

The largest known comet tail is 560 million km (348 million mi) long and belongs to Comet Hyakutake.

WHAT DID THE FIRST ASTRONAUTS EAT?

The first astronauts weren't equipped with hot water to rehydrate food, so they ate small, dry cubes of food or meals they squeezed out of tubes.

WHAT FOOD WON'T FLOAT AWAY IN SPACE?

In space, yogurt will still stay on a spoon, where other foods will float off and drift around the spaceship.

WHAT ARE ASTRONAUT TOILETS LIKE?

Space lavatories have straps for the astronauts' feet and thighs to stop them from drifting off the toilet halfway through!

WHAT HAPPENS WHEN YOU SWEAT IN SPACE?

NASA—the National Aeronautics and Space Administration, founded in the USA in 1958—has developed ways to collect sweat from exercising astronauts to convert into drinking water for them in space. They can also do this with urine!

DO ASTRONAUTS WEAR DIAPERS?

Astronauts wear diapers during takeoff, landing, and on space walks, as they can't go to the lavatory at these times!

WHO HAS BEEN IN SPACE THE LONGEST?

Russian cosmonaut Gennady Padalka holds the current record for time in Earth orbit. His time spent aboard Mir and the International Space Station adds up to an incredible 879 days.

HAS A DOG BEEN INTO SPACE?

In 1957, a stray dog called Laika became the first dog in space. She went on the satellite Sputnik 2 launched by the USSR, but died in space because the satellite had no means of returning to Earth.

WHAT IS THE VOMIT COMET?

The "Vomit Comet" is the name given to an aircraft that flies in such a way that it produces weightlessness. It's used to train astronauts, carry out research, and even make movies. It tends to make people sick, as you could probably guess ...

WHAT ARE THE EFFECTS OF ZERO GRAVITY?

The effects of zero gravity on the human body are so severe that astronauts who stay in space for a long time suffer muscle wasting and loss of bone density. They can be unwell for months or sometimes years after their return to Earth.

WHAT HAPPENS TO POOP IN SPACE?

On the International Space Station, all waste from the lavatories is stored in a supply craft called The Progress. The craft is eventually released and burns away in Earth's atmosphere. Solid waste from space lavatories on shuttles is compressed and stored for return to Earth; liquid waste is thrown out into space.

HOW DO ASTRONAUTS WASH THEIR HAIR?

Astronauts use special shampoo that they don't have to wash out of their hair.

WHEN DID THE LAST ASTRONAUT WALK ON THE MOON?

The last time a human stepped on the Moon was in December 1972.

WHERE DO ASTRONAUTS TRAIN?

NASA uses part of the Arizona desert, USA, to train astronauts. The heat and dust storms make it unpleasant, but the harsh environment is ideal for trying out new equipment and techniques.

DID YOU KNOW?

Astronauts have to spend time in quarantine before and after they go into space.

WHAT DOES THE INTERNATIONAL SPACE STATION USE FOR POWER?

The International Space Station is equipped with huge solar panels and all its power comes from the Sun.

WHERE CAN YOU HEAR WHALES IN SPACE?

The Voyager spacecrafts carry gold-plated disks containing images and sounds from Earth. They include spoken greetings in 55 languages, including an ancient language not spoken for 6,000 years. They also contain whale music and other animal sounds—so any aliens listening to it might think that humans all talk in "whale!"

CAN SPACESHIPS USE PLANETS TO SPEED UP?

To get up to speed without using fuel, spacecraft often use the gravity of planets as a sort of slingshot—the spaceship whizzes around the planet and is thrown out into space. It's called a "gravity assist" move.

DID YOU KNOW?

A spacecraft powered by photons (light particles) would build up to a speed of 160,934 km (100,000 mi) per hour after three years.

WHEN WILL THE PIONEER SPACECRAFT REACH A STAR?

NASA's Pioneer spacecraft was launched in 1972 on its voyage toward the star Aldebaran, but will take two million years to arrive! Its last contact with Earth was in 2003.

WHERE IS THE NEAREST STAR AFTER THE SUN?

Apart from the Sun, our closest star, Proxima Centauri, is 40 trillion km (25 trillion mi) from Earth. This is 4.24 light years.

DID YOU KNOW?

The International Space Station can be seen orbiting the Earth with the naked eye! The best time to look for it is after sunset.

HAS ANYONE SEEN A STAR EXPLODE?

The Crab Nebula is an area of really bright gas and was formed by an exploding star. The explosion was seen by Chinese astronomers in 1054 and was bright enough to be seen with the naked eye in daylight for 23 days after that. The debris from the Crab Nebula explosion is still making its way through the universe at 1,800 km/s (1,100 mps).

DID YOU KNOW?

The star Alpha Herculis is 25 times larger than the diameter of the Earth's orbit around the Sun.

WHAT IS A WHITE DWARF?

A white dwarf is the leftover middle of a star that has used up all its nuclear fuel. As they get older, white dwarves keep on getting cooler and can crystallize to form gigantic diamonds!

IS THERE A DIAMOND IN SPACE?

In 2004, astronomers discovered a white dwarf that had turned into a huge diamond! It measures 4,000 km (2,485 mi) across and if it were sold, it would have 10 billion, trillion, trillion carats!

IS THERE A REAL DEATH STAR?

Some astronomers believe there may be a brown dwarf (a medium-size space object) orbiting at more than 50,000 times the Earth's distance from the Sun. It has been named Nemesis or "death star."

DID YOU KNOW?

There are 100 billion stars in a typical galaxy.

WHAT IS A BLACK HOLE?

A black hole is an area in space with a gravitational field that is so strong, that nothing inside it can ever escape—not even light—which is how they got their rather dark name. If you managed to get within 161 km (100 mi) of a black hole, you'd be heated up to over 2,000,000 degrees Celsius (3,600,000 degrees Fahrenheit)!

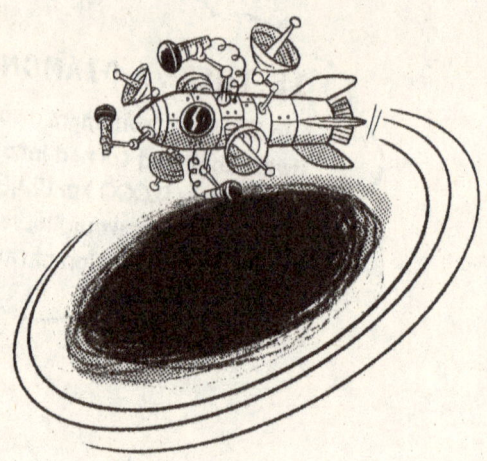

DID YOU KNOW?

The most distant black hole that we know of is 13 billion light years away. It weighs three billion times as much as the Sun.

CAN YOU HEAR BLACK HOLES?

Black holes can "sing." A black hole in the Perseus galaxy, 250 million light years away, has been emitting an extremely low musical sound for two billion years. X-rays can detect it, but we can't hear it.

WHAT WOULD HAPPEN IF YOU FELL INTO A BLACK HOLE?

If you fell into a black hole, your body would be "spaghettified"—drawn out into an incredibly long, thin strand. If you managed to fall right into a black hole and stay conscious, you may carry on falling forever—time effectively stands still, so you'd never get to the bottom!

HOW MANY GALAXIES ARE THERE?

There are hundreds of billions of galaxies in the universe ... too many to count, in fact!

DID YOU KNOW?

The size of the universe is so vast compared to the matter it contains that it's equivalent to a box, measuring 32 km (20 mi) in all dimensions, containing one grain of sand.

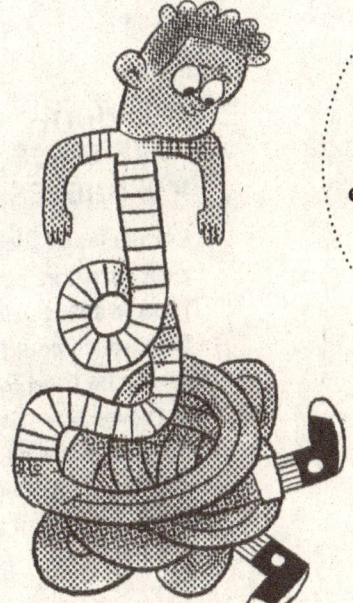

WHAT IS MOST OF THE UNIVERSE MADE OF?

Most of the mass of the universe (96 percent) is made up of mysterious "dark matter" that we can't see at all and know nothing about ...

WHAT IS THE COLDEST TEMPERATURE POSSIBLE?

The coldest temperature possible is called absolute zero. It is minus 273.15 degrees Celsius (minus 459.67 degrees Fahrenheit) and is the temperature at which atoms and molecules stop moving.

WHAT ARE SPACE WORMHOLES?

Wormholes (if they exist) are tunnels through space and time, which could possibly be used for time travel. Scientists think wormholes may be so tiny that they are narrower than a single atom.

COULD ALIENS BE LISTENING TO US?

Aliens on distant planets could pick up human radio broadcasts from 80 years ago. Radio travels at the speed of light, so broadcasts from 80 years ago will now be reaching planets 80 light years from Earth. If aliens living on planets only 40 light years away have sent a reply, it will arrive any day now!

HAVE WE EVER RECEIVED A MESSAGE FROM ALIENS?

A radio signal from space, known as the "Wow!" signal, has never been explained and could be real evidence of intelligent life. It was picked up in 1977 but has never been repeated.

CAN TIME MOVE SLOWER?

Time moves slower near things that exert a lot of gravitational force, such as large stars.

WHAT HAPPENS TO LIQUIDS IN SPACE?

In space, all liquids (including urine) simultaneously boil and freeze. A liquid that is spilled or dumped into outer space instantly spreads out into a mist, and then the droplets freeze into a fine haze of ice crystals.

HOW FAR IS A LIGHT YEAR?

A light year is the distance that light can travel in one year. It works out at about 9 trillion km (6 trillion mi)!

DID YOU KNOW?

Every atom in your body was once part of a star.

STRANGE SCIENCE

HOW MANY GRAINS OF SAND WOULD FIT INTO A CUP?

An average-sized teacup can hold around one million grains of sand.

DID YOU KNOW?

Rubber bands last longer if they are kept in a refrigerator.

HOW FAR COULD YOU DRAW WITH A PENCIL?

There is enough lead in a pencil to draw a line that is 56 km (35 mi) long. You'd need a good pencil sharpener though!

HOW FAST IS A COUCH?

Marek Turowski from the UK reached a speed of 148 km/h (92 mph) driving a motorized couch in May 2007.

IS THERE SUCH A THING AS AN INVISIBILITY CLOAK?

Scientists are working on a "cloak of invisibility" that will hide objects by making light waves flow around them, like water flowing around a rock in a river.

WHY DOES KETCHUP GET STUCK IN A BOTTLE?

There's a reason why tomato ketchup won't come out of the bottle and then falls out in a huge dollop—it's called shear thinning. Some thick liquids go thin when shaken, but no one knows exactly how it works and scientists can't predict when it will happen.

WHAT IS EARTHRACE?

Earthrace is said to be the world's fastest eco boat. It's partly powered by human fat from its crew members!

COULD YOU BOUNCE LIGHT OFF THE MOON?

A laser is a very narrow beam of powerful light. It is so straight that it doesn't spread out evenly over huge distances. A laser beam could be reflected off a mirror on the Moon and return back to Earth in a straight line.

DID YOU KNOW?

It's impossible to fold a dry piece of paper in half more than seven times. Give it a try!

WHAT METAL WOULD MELT IN YOUR HAND?

The metal gallium melts at body heat—if you held a piece in your hand, it would gradually melt into a pool of liquid.

HAS THERE EVER BEEN A ROBOT ZOO?

Robotarium X in Portugal was the first zoo full of robots, where 45 robots shared a steel and glass cage. Some were nice and responded to visitors. Others were nasty and bit the tails of their companions. How bizarre!

CAN VULTURES SMELL GAS?

When a gas pipeline leaks in the California desert, workers put a chemical into the gas that attracts turkey vultures. The vultures gather where the gas leaks out, so workers only need to spot the turkey vultures to find the leak.

HOW DO YOU MAKE A POISON ARROW?

Some tribes in the Amazon rain forest heat poison arrow frogs over a fire to sweat the poison out of them. They use the poison to tip their hunting arrows.

DID YOU KNOW?

Recycling one plastic bottle saves enough energy to power a 60-watt light bulb for six hours.

IS STRIPED TOOTHPASTE BETTER FOR YOUR TEETH?

There is no benefit in using striped toothpaste—the stripes just make the toothpaste look more interesting.

CAN YOU DAMAGE A MAGNET?

Dropping, heating, or hammering a magnet can reduce its magnetic power.

DID YOU KNOW?

The National Institute for Standards and Technology in the USA has made an atomic clock as small as a grain of rice.

CAN CATS MAKE ELECTRICITY?

If you were to stroke a cat 70 million times, you would generate enough static electricity to power a 60-watt light bulb for one minute. Don't try this one at home ... the poor cat would have no hair left!

DO SMARTPHONES FRIGHTEN GHOSTS?

Reports of ghosts have dropped considerably as the use of smartphones has increased. It seems that the ghouls don't like the radio waves!

CAN BLUE LIGHTS KEEP YOU AWAKE?

Scientists are testing the use of blue lights to help keep night drivers awake. They work by convincing the human body clock that it's morning!

DID YOU KNOW?

Liquid helium will crawl up the sides of its container if the top is warmer than the bottom.

CAN YOU HOLD WATER IN AN UPSIDE-DOWN BUCKET?

If you whirl a bucket of water around fast enough, the water will not fall out even when the bucket is upside down! This happens because the centrifugal force (that pushes objects outwards) is greater than the force of gravity, which would normally cause the water to fall.

WHO INVENTED THE MICROWAVE OVEN?

Percy Spencer (USA) invented the microwave oven in 1945, using new technology developed for military defence during the Second World War.

DID YOU KNOW?

If a glass of water were magnified to the size of the whole Earth, each molecule would be the size of a tennis ball.

CAN WATER CLIMB?

If an electric current is applied to two glasses of water standing next to each other, with the positive electrode in one glass and the negative in the other, the water will climb up the walls of the glass and form a bridge between the two glasses in midair to allow the current to flow.

DID YOU KNOW?

The longest journey ever made on a tractor was 25,378 km (15,769 mi) in Germany in 2016.

HOW WERE CATFISH USED BY DOCTORS?

Doctors in ancient Egypt would give patients an electric shock with a catfish to treat the pain caused by arthritis.

WHY DOES COOKING GAS SMELL?

The gas used for cookers and fires has no smell. The gas supply company adds the strong smell deliberately so people can tell immediately if there is a leak.

DO WE BRUSH OUR TEETH WITH SKELETONS?

Many types of toothpaste contain the skeletons of microscopic creatures from the sea, called diatoms.

DID YOU KNOW?

Antifreeze is deadly poisonous—some governments insist that manufacturers add a chemical to make it taste horrible to stop people and animals from drinking it.

WHAT ARE BLACK LIGHT BULBS?

Black light bulbs emit light in the ultraviolet range of the spectrum.

DID YOU KNOW?

Many people believe that human bodies decay slower than they used to as food is now packed with preservatives that make their way into the flesh—and preserve us too!

CAN PEOPLE EAT ROCKS?

Salt is the only rock that humans can eat.

HOW ARE THE HOLES IN CHEESE MADE?

Bubbles of gas produced by bacteria form the holes in Swiss cheese.

DID YOU KNOW?

In terms of its size, a laser is a brighter light than the Sun.

WHO INVENTED CONCRETE?

Roman engineers were ahead of their time. They heated chalk and seashells at over 900 degrees Celsius (1,650 degrees Fahrenheit) to make lime, to which they added volcanic ash, to make concrete.

DID YOU KNOW?

An Australian scientist started a long experiment in 1927 to prove that pitch (a sticky black substance used for waterproofing boats and roofs) is not solid, but a very thick liquid. He put some pitch in a glass funnel and left it to drip through—by 1995, only seven drops had fallen through the funnel!

DO SLUGS WORK LIKE BATTERIES?

The slime produced by a slug produces a small electric current when smeared over copper. Slug-powered phone, anyone?

DID YOU KNOW?

Diamonds are made from the same chemical as the lead in pencils, but the atoms are arranged differently.

DO SHARKS SLEEP?

Not all of them! Many species of sharks need to keep moving forward all the time in order to push water over their gills, otherwise they won't be able to breathe. This means that only part of their brain will "sleep" at any time.

WHERE WILL PIGEONS REFUSE TO LAND?

Pigeons won't land on a statue that contains the metal gallium. A Japanese scientist is developing a spray containing gallium that can be used to treat buildings to keep them free from bird droppings.

DID YOU KNOW?

The world's highest limousine was built in Australia and measures 3.33 m (10 ft 11 in) from floor to roof. It took 4,000 hours to build.

DOES KRYPTONITE EXIST?

Scientists have discovered kryptonite (the fictional mineral supposed to deprive Superman of his powers) in a mine in Serbia. The mineral, called sodium lithium boron silicate hydroxide, exactly matches the formula of kryptonite in the film *Superman Returns*.

DID YOU KNOW?

Plastic can take up to 500 years to decompose.

CAN BUBBLES FREEZE?

At temperatures below about minus 25 degrees Celsius (minus 13 degrees Fahrenheit), soap bubbles can freeze in the air and shatter when hitting the ground.

WHAT IS FASTER—LIGHT OR SOUND?

Sound travels through air at a millionth of the speed of light, which is why you see lightning flash before you hear thunder.

WHAT DOES A SMART TOOTHBRUSH DO?

A smart toothbrush uses wireless technology to send information to a screen that can be stuck on a bathroom mirror. The toothbrush monitors and reports back on how well you are brushing and if you've missed any bits!

DID YOU KNOW?

Some types of rubber can be stretched to 1,000 times their original length.

WHAT WAS THE GRIMMEST JOB IN THE WORLD?

French scientist Antoine-Francois Fourcroy had the lovely job of studying the effects of heat, air, water, and other chemicals on rotting corpses.

CAN OXYGEN FREEZE?

Oxygen turns to a blue liquid at minus 183 degrees Celsius (minus 297 degrees Fahrenheit). It freezes to a solid at minus 218 degrees Celsius (minus 362 degrees Fahrenheit).

DID YOU KNOW?

An echo is a sound reflection. To hear an echo, the sound must bounce off a surface that's at least 17 m (56 ft) away. The echo still happens at closer distances, but it comes back too quickly for your ear to hear it.

HOW BIG WERE THE FIRST COMPUTERS?

The first computers used to be so big that they would take up a whole room! By the 1960s, the electronic parts were getting smaller, so they gradually shrank in size. Today, computers can be so tiny that they can fit in the palm of your hand!

DID YOU KNOW?

Recycling one glass bottle saves enough energy to power a computer for 25 minutes.

HOW WAS PEE USED TO LIGHT MATCHES?

Phosphorous (the chemical used for making matches) was first created when chemists extracted it from their urine. The urine was left to stand until it putrefied (went bad). It was later extracted from burned and crushed bones.

CAN YOU MAKE A MAGNET?

Any magnetic material that is touching a magnet starts to behave like a magnet too! If you attach a paper clip to a magnet, you'll discover that you can attach another one to the first paper clip ... then another ... as many as you like! If you then break the first clip's contact with the real magnet, they will all fall off and lose their "stolen" magnetism!

IS DRINKING WATER SECOND-HAND?

Drinking water has been through many other people's bodies before it gets to you. But don't worry—it's been cleaned!

DID YOU KNOW?

A Hungarian called Ladislo Biro invented the first ballpoint pen in 1938.

HOW DO YOU MAKE FERTILIZER?

A traditional old recipe for plant fertilizer consisted of rotten cow dung, ground-up bones, and dry blood. In fact, you can still buy any or all of these or make your own. Or you could just buy a bottle of fertilizer ...

WHAT MAKES BLUE CHEESE SMELLY?

The fungus that gives Stilton cheese its special smell and taste is related to penicillin, an antibiotic that you may take when you're ill.

WHAT IS A NANOSWIMMER?

Scientists are trying to make nanoswimmers—tiny devices that can swim through blood vessels to keep people healthy or cure illness.

CAN AIR GUITARS MAKE SOUNDS?

An electronic air guitar device can pick up the movements of your pretend guitar playing and translate them into real guitar sounds.

DID THE BRITISH DESTROY THEIR BEST COMPUTERS?

The first programmable computer, Colossus, was built in England during World War II to crack coded enemy messages. All 14 Colossus computers were destroyed after the war, and the British government denied they had ever existed.

DID YOU KNOW?

Tall buildings are built not to wobble in the wind—but this isn't for safety, it's purely for comfort. People feel unsafe if they can see water sloshing around in the toilet!

CAN CARS PLAY TUNES?

Roads in Japan are being built with grooves cut in them so that if cars drive over them at the right speed, they play a tune!

DID YOU KNOW?

Arsenic was so commonly used as a poison by murderers in the 1800s that a law was passed in Britain in 1840 that arsenic must be mixed with a blue or black dye so people could see it in their food. It might have been better to stop pharmacists from selling it ...

ARE THERE REALLY MAGNET-POWERED TRAINS?

Yes! Maglev trains are able to run at a speed of up to 400 km/h (248 mph). The trains aren't attached to the rails ... they're just pulled along by magnetic force.

WHO IS THE WORLD'S WEIRDEST ARTIST?

German doctor Gunther von Hagens preserves dead bodies and organs for art. He uses a process called plastination to replace body fluids with plastic. The bodies are shown in art exhibitions and used as learning aids for trainee doctors.

DID YOU KNOW?

If you dip a flower into liquid nitrogen, it freezes instantly and becomes so brittle that you can smash it with a hammer.

WHAT IS THE DEEPEST HOLE EVER DUG?

The deepest hole ever dug by humans is in the Kola Peninsula in Russia—the drilling was completed in 1989. It was 12.3 km (7.6 mi) deep.